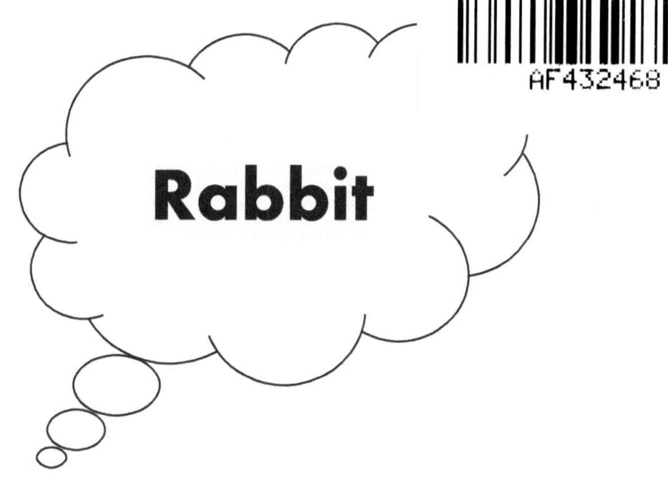
Rabbit

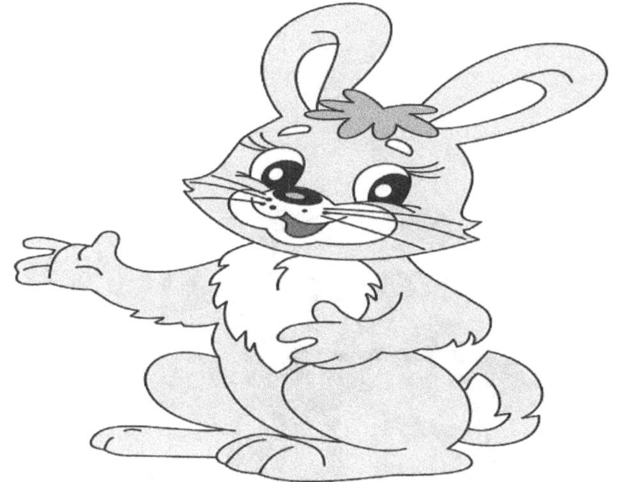

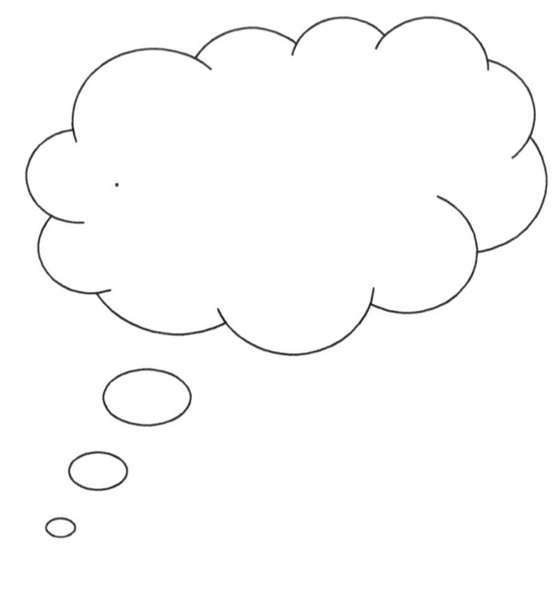

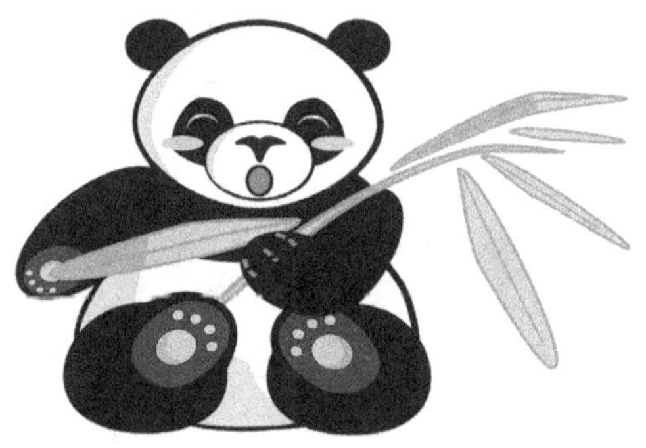

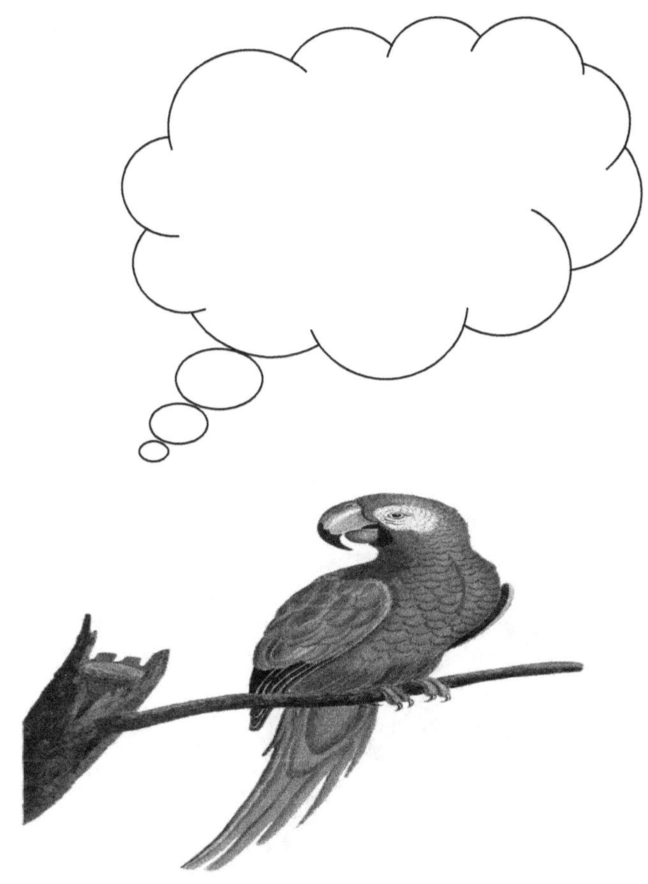

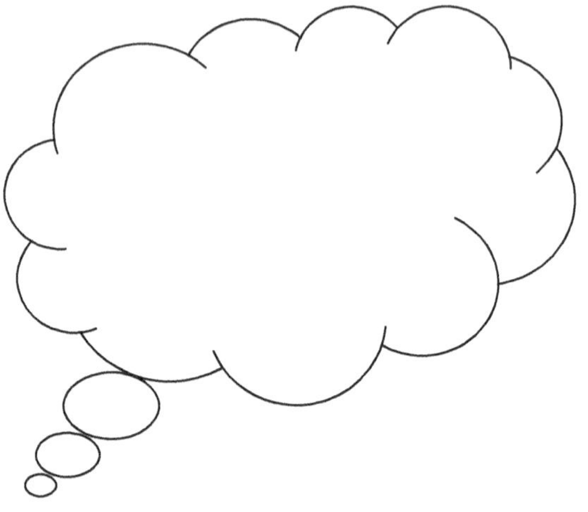

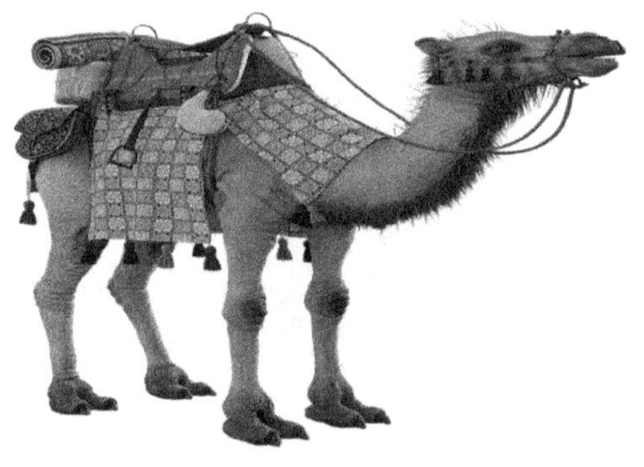

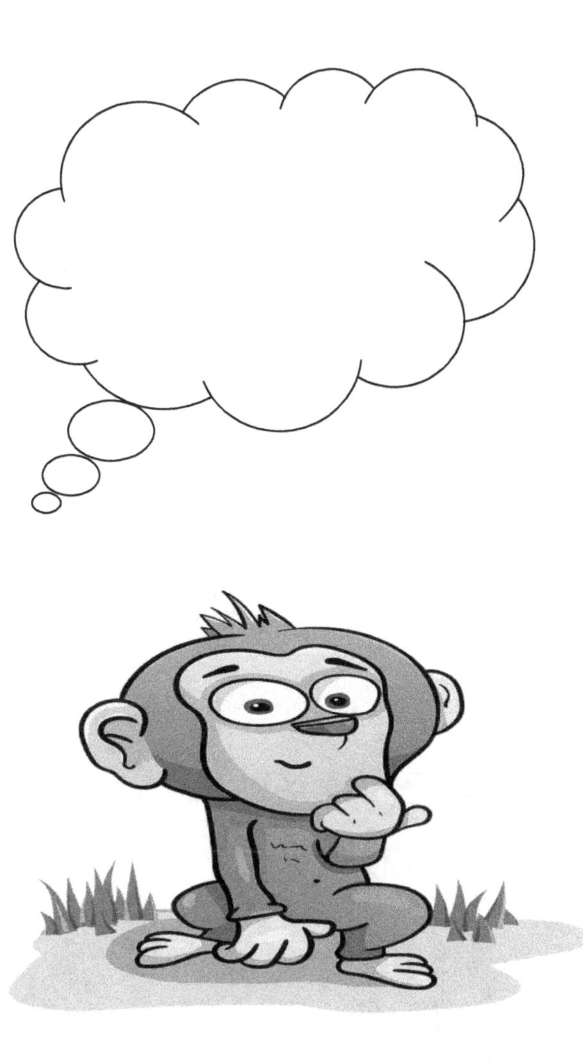

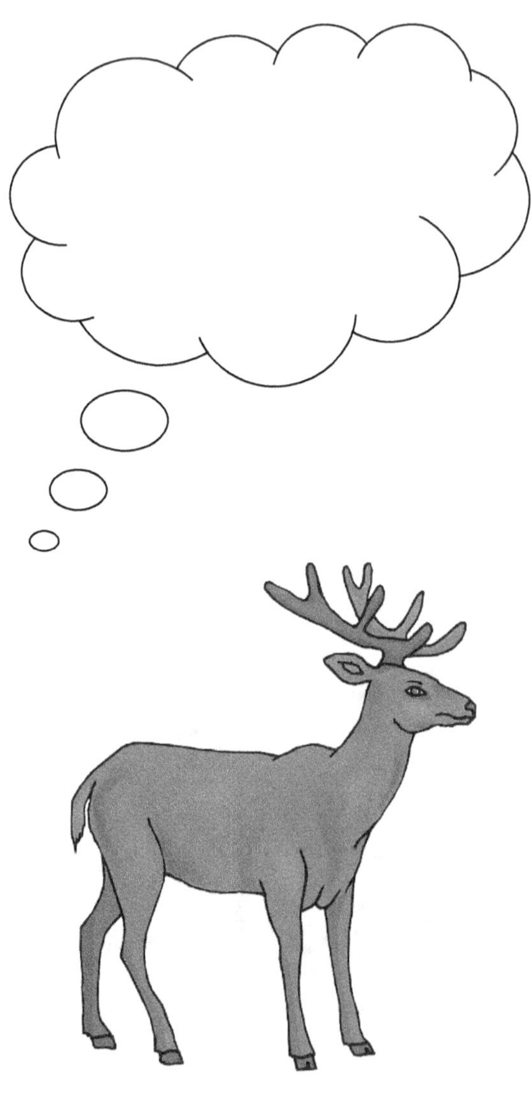

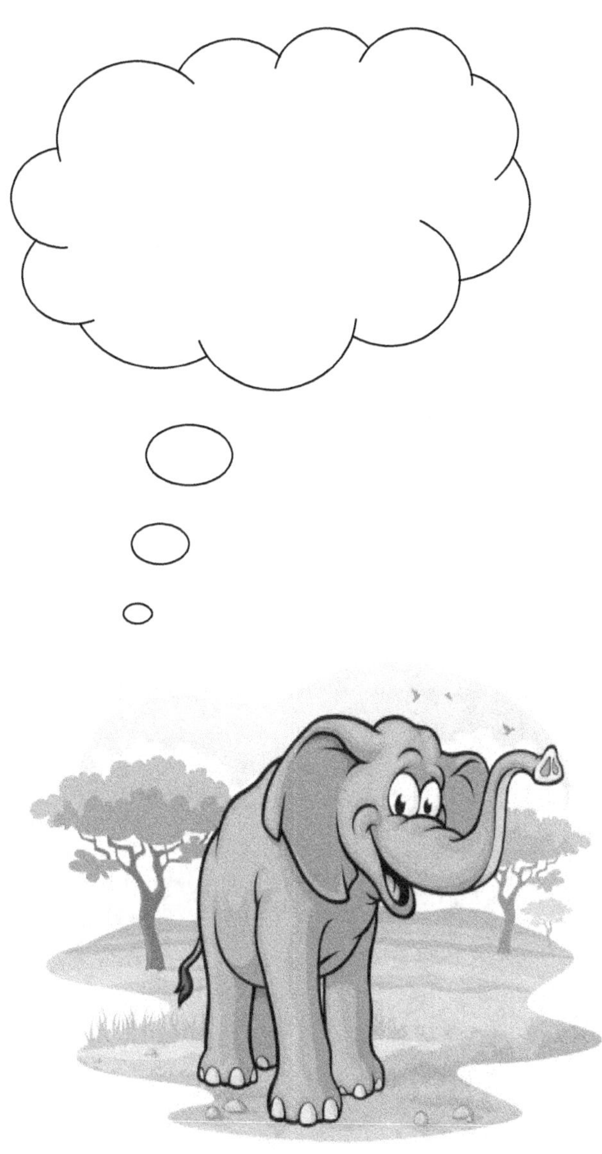

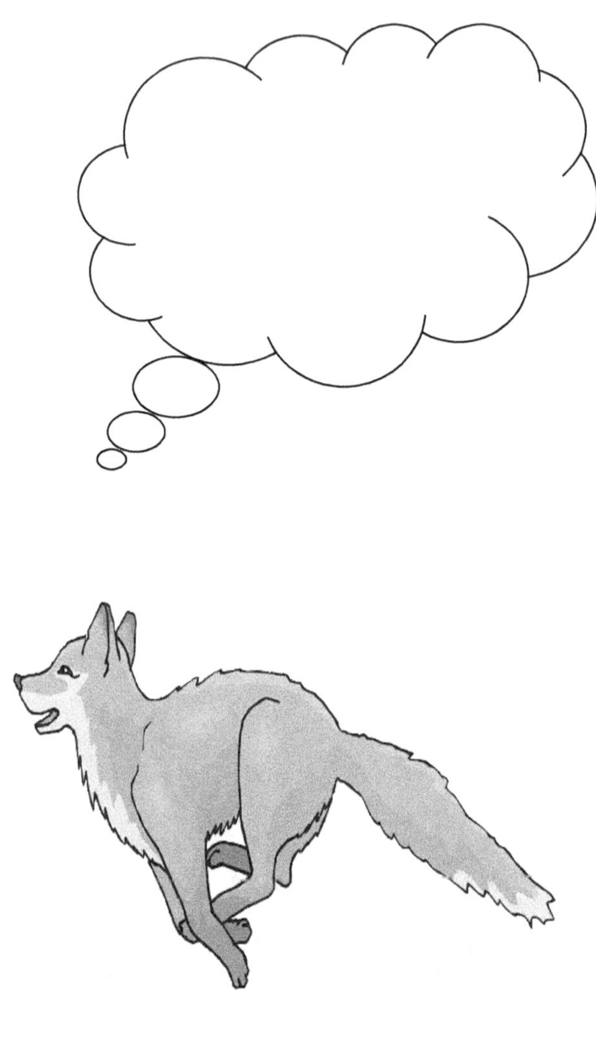

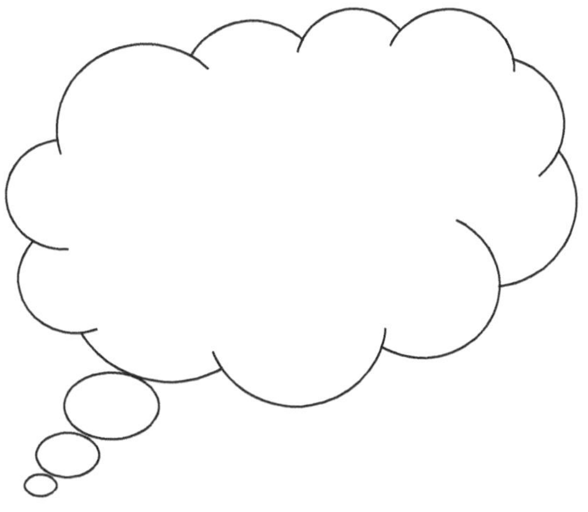
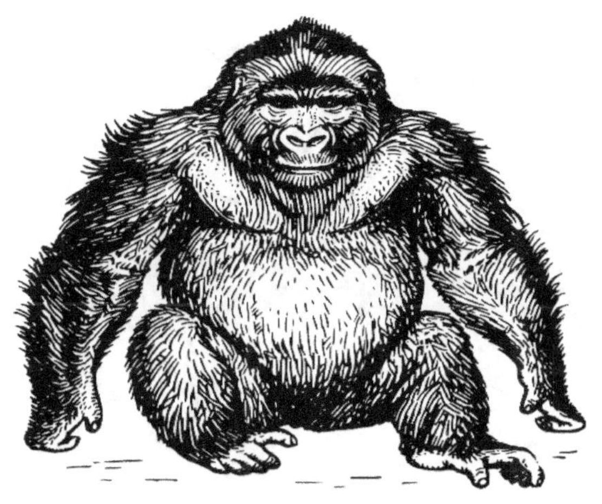

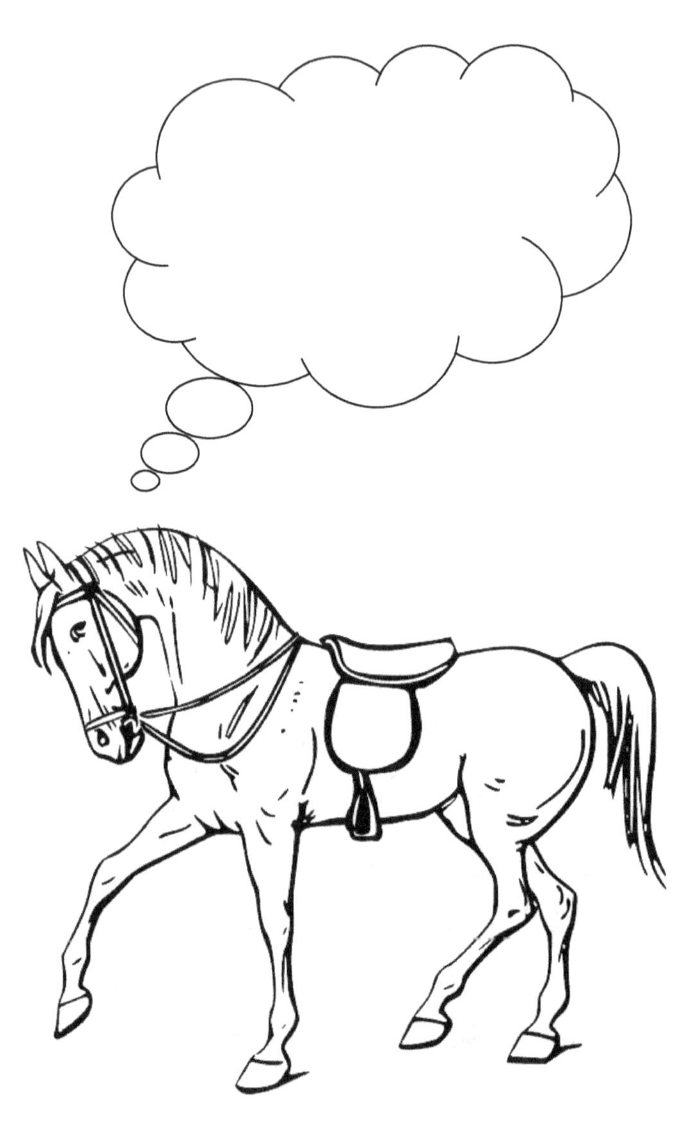

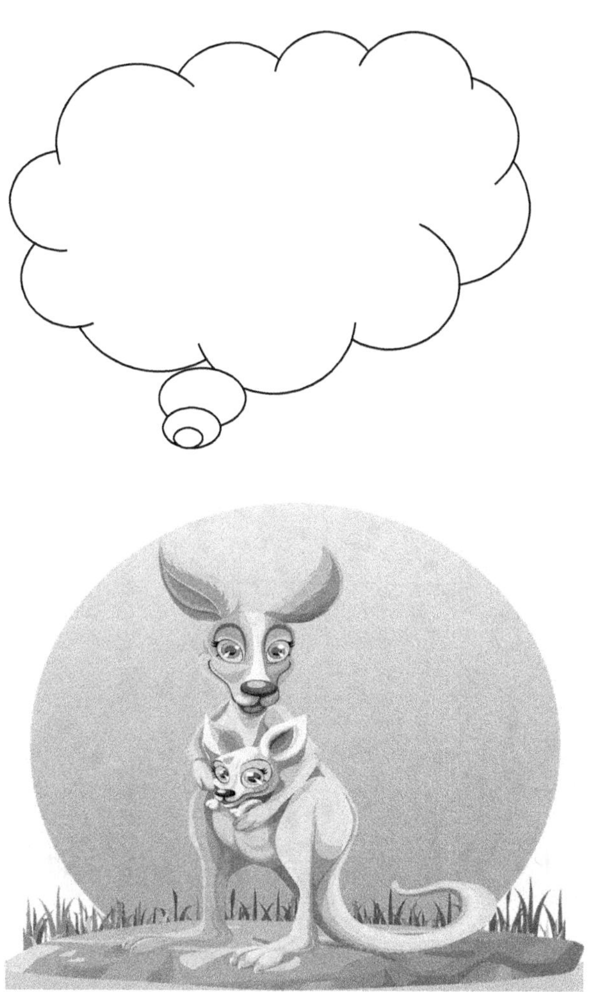

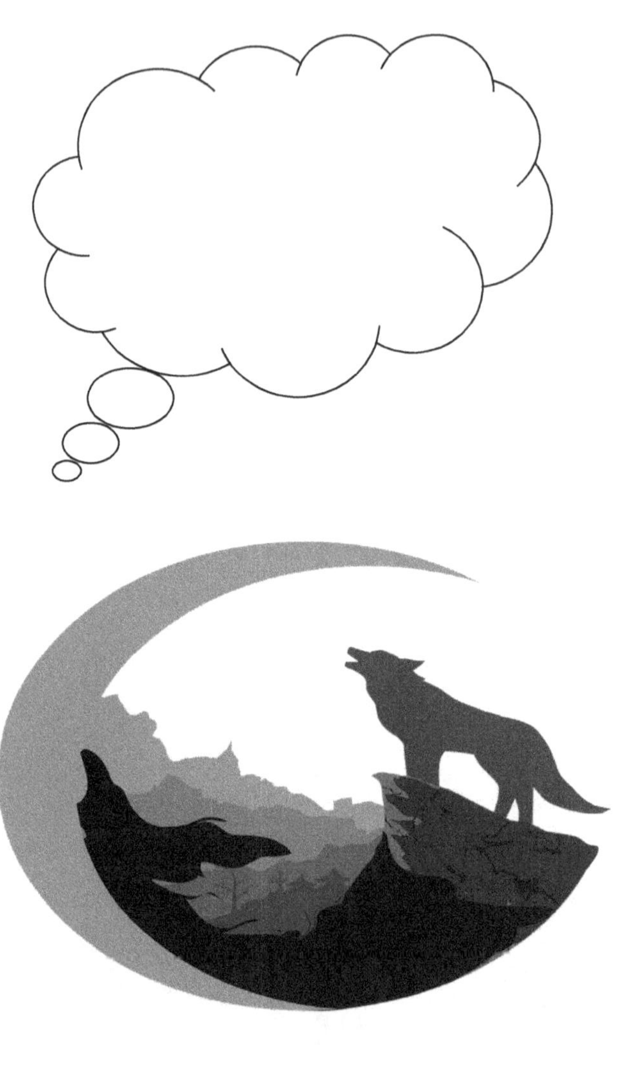

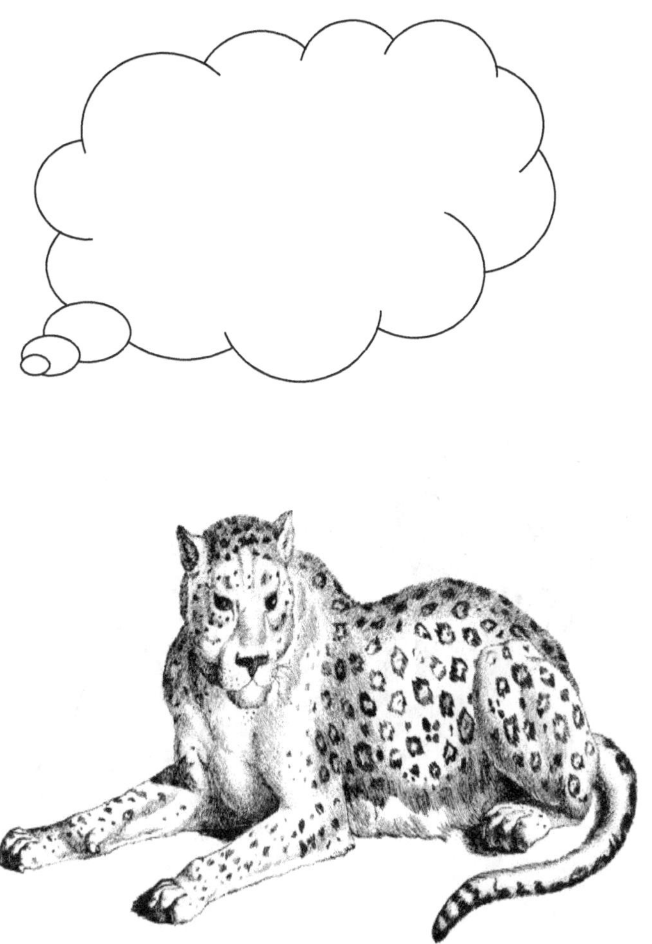

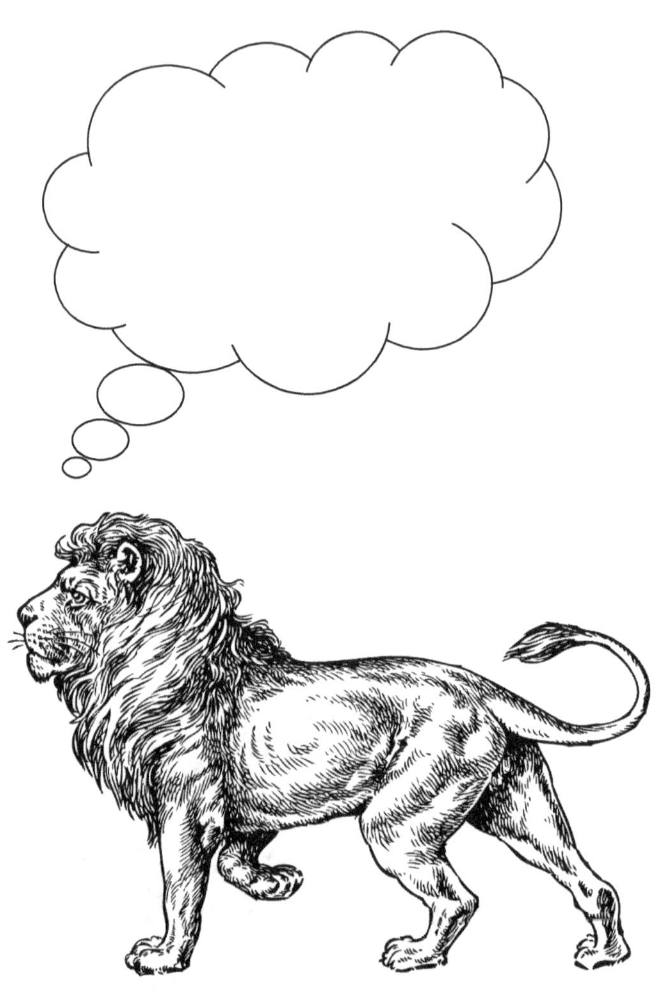

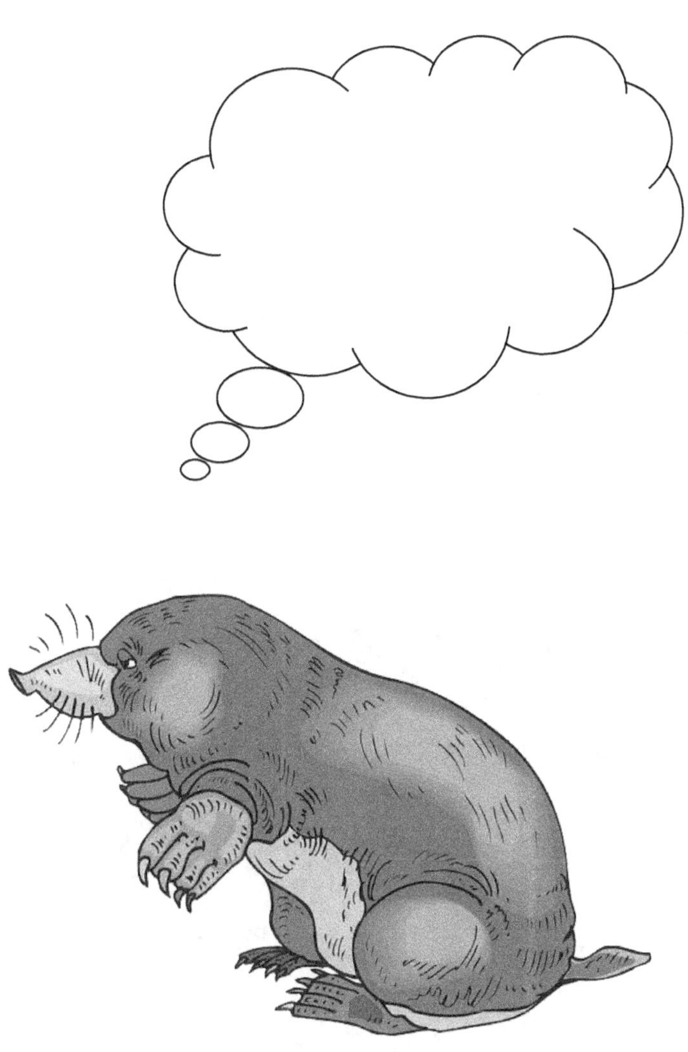

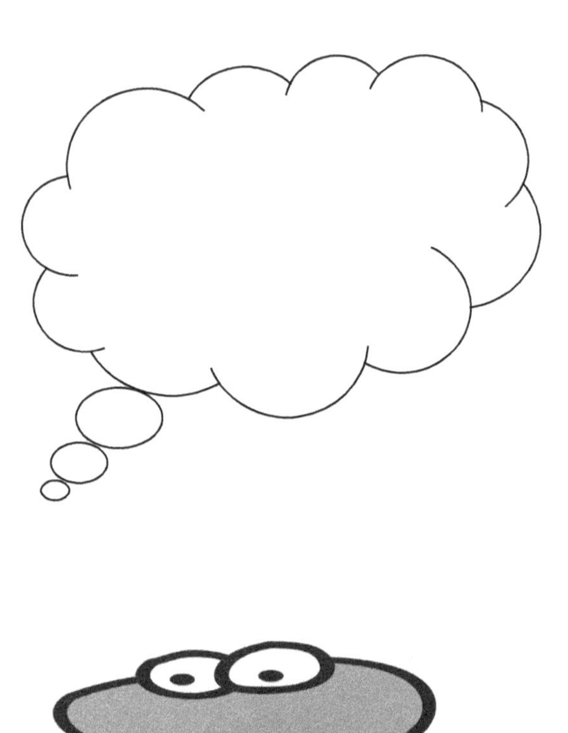

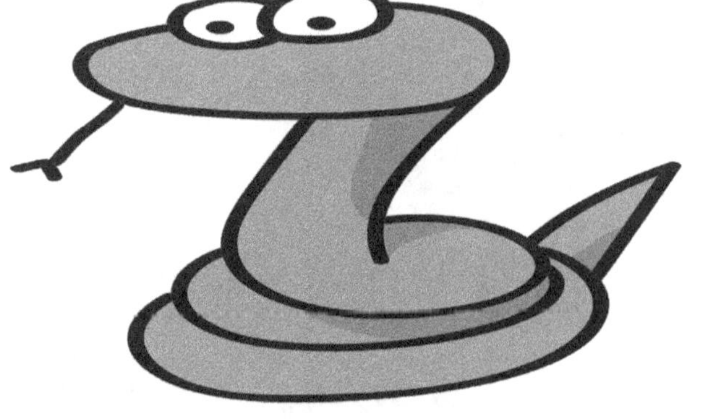

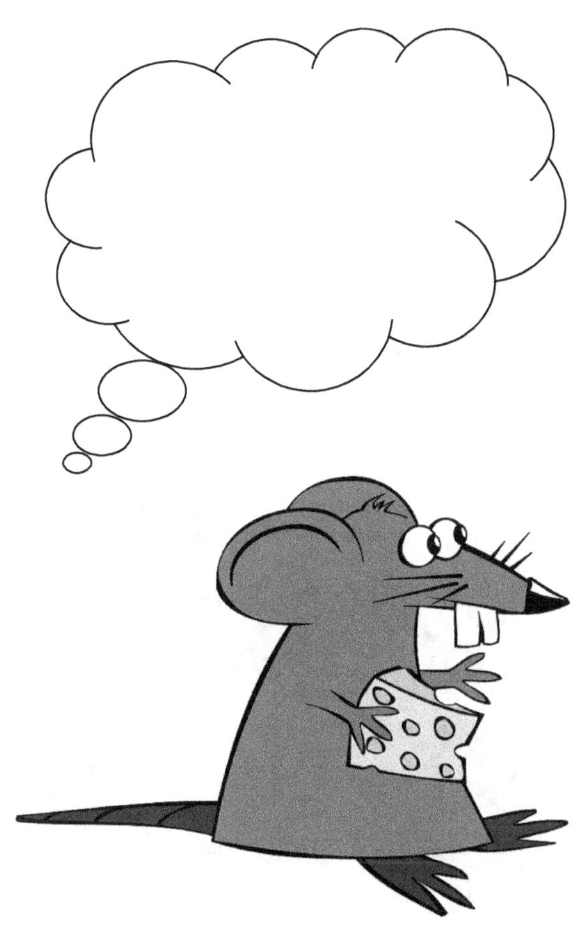

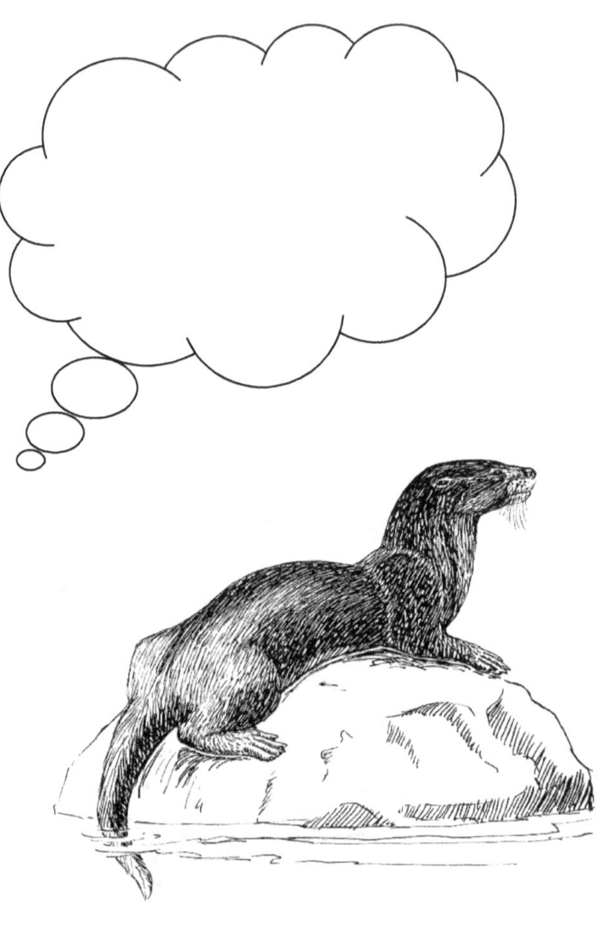

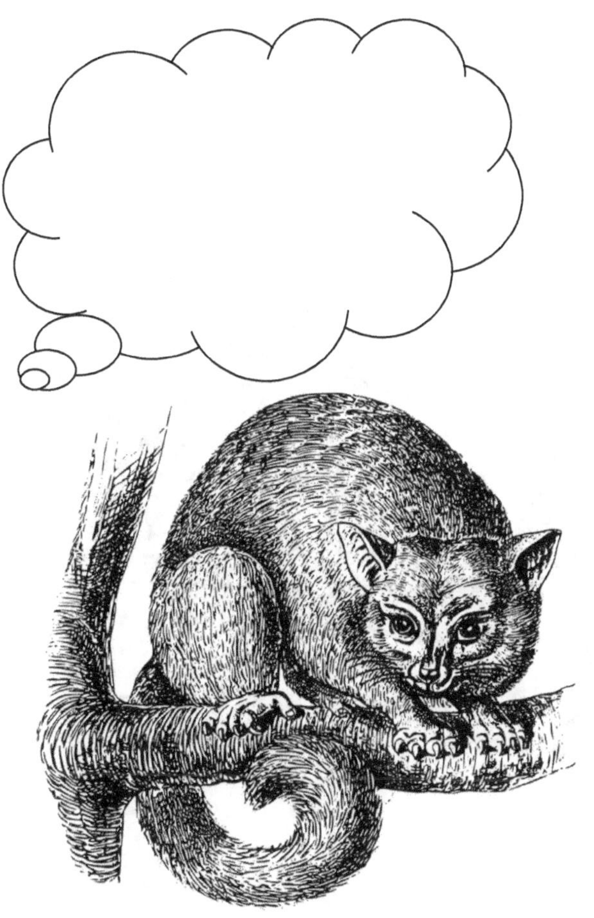

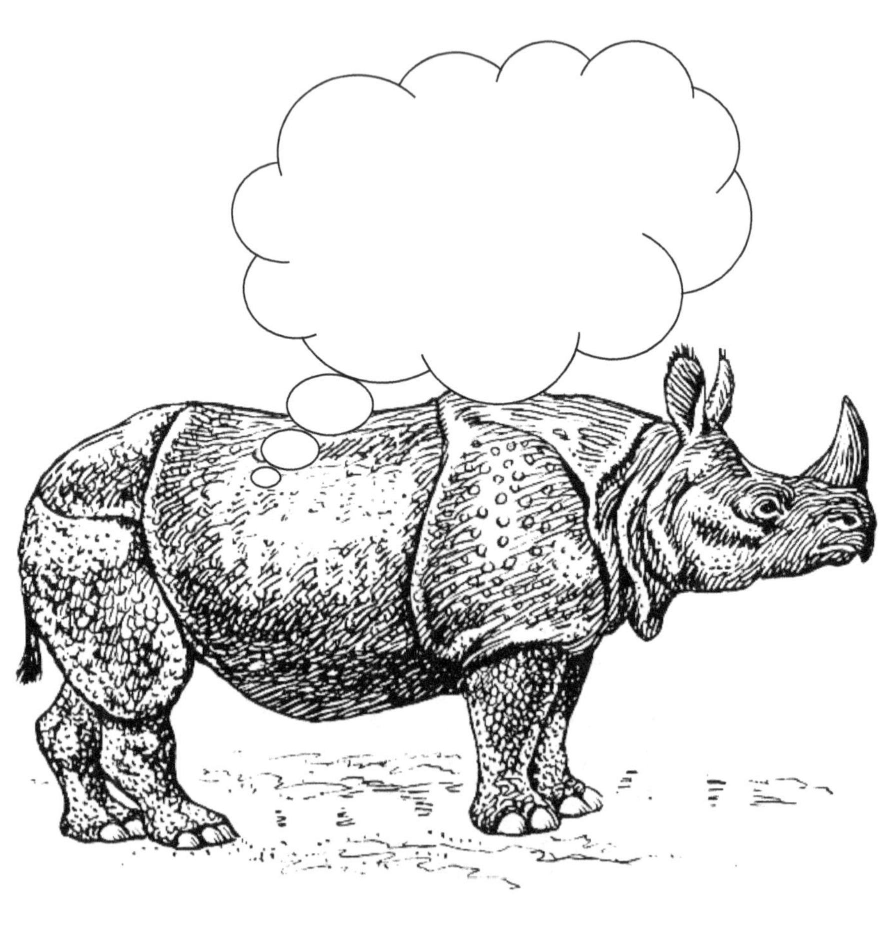

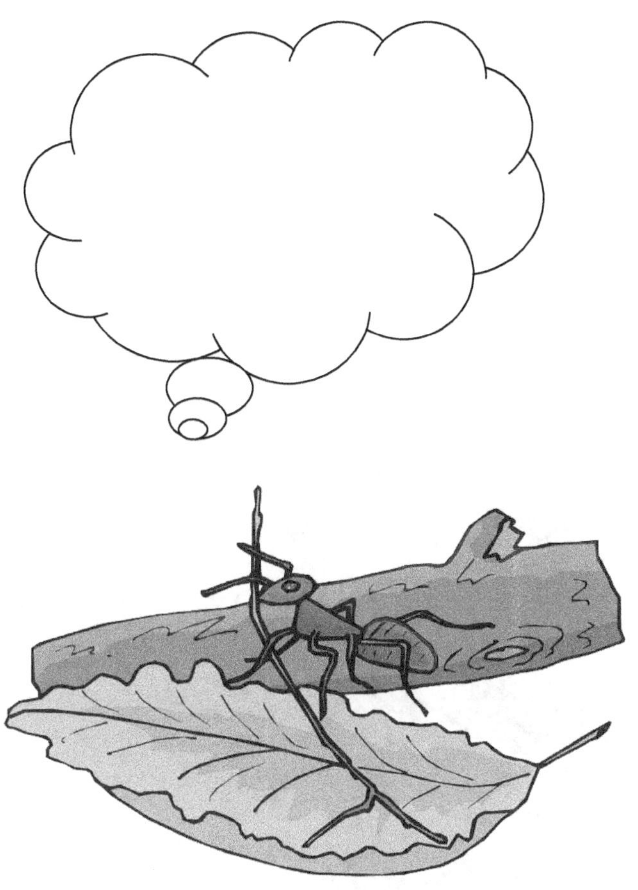

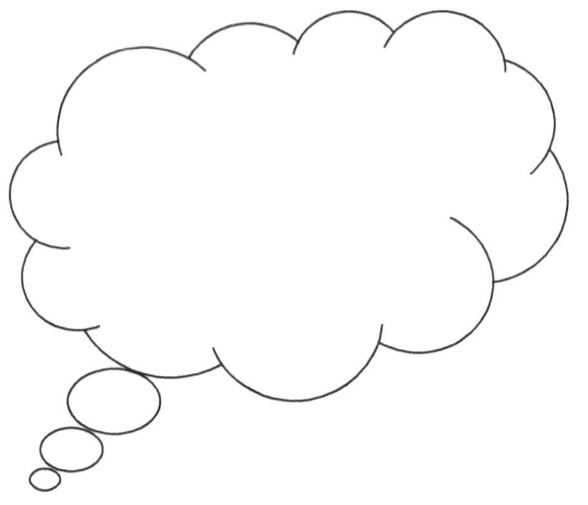

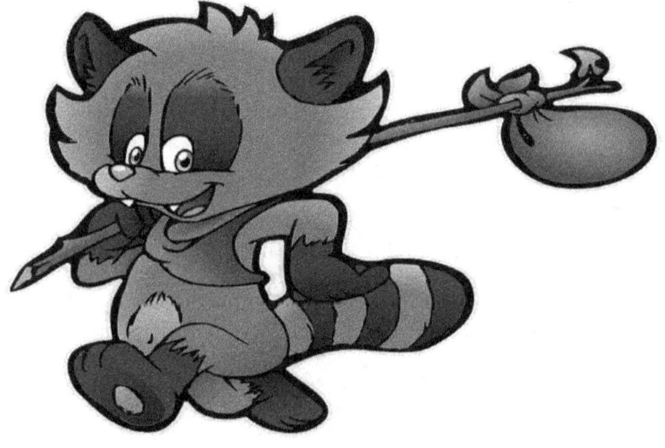

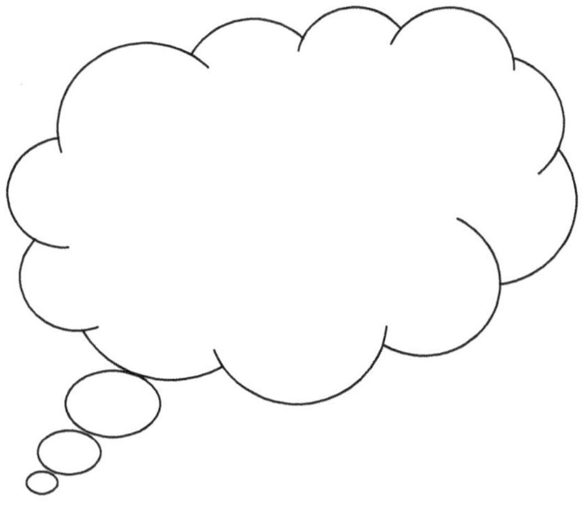

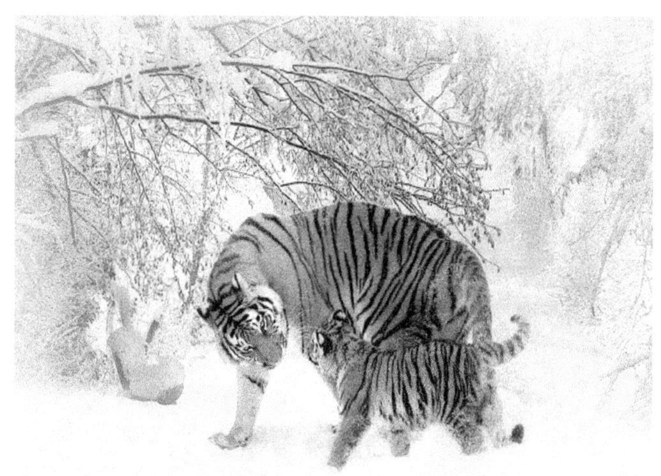

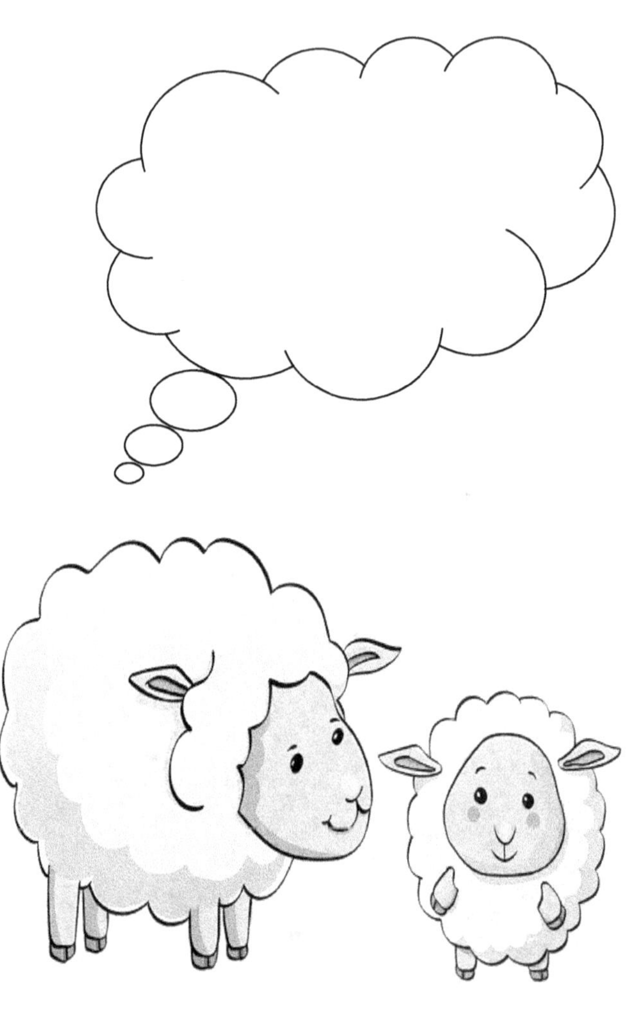

What is your favorite animal?

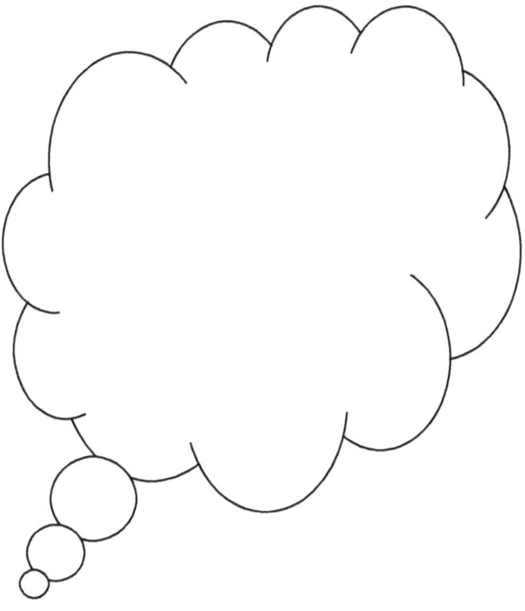